INTRODUCTION TO
BIOLOGY

Jane Chisholm and David Beeson
Consultant editor: Alan Alder
Designed by Iain Ashman and Roger Priddy

Illustrated by Sue Stitt, Kuo Kang Chen, Graham Round,
Chris Shields, Ian Jackson, Aziz Khan, Chris Lyon,
David Quinn, Martin Newton and Rob McCaig.

Computer program by Christopher Smith

Program edited by Chris Oxlade

WITH COMPUTER PROGRAM LISTING

Contents

First published in 1984 by
Usborne Publishing Ltd, 20 Garrick Street,
London WC2E 9BJ, England.

Copyright © 1984 Usborne Publishing.
The name Usborne and the device ⲟⲾⲂⲞⲢⲚⲈ are
Trade Marks of Usborne Publishing Ltd. All

Printed in Spain

What is biology?

Biology is the study of all living things. It comes from two Greek words, *bios*, meaning "life", and *logos*, meaning "knowledge". Biology can be divided into lots of different branches.

Zoology is the study of animals.

Botany is the study of plants.

Ecology deals with the relationship between living things and the world around them.

Some biologists concentrate on life in a particular setting. The study of living things in the sea is called marine biology.

Others specialize in a particular kind of animal or plant. For instance, ornithologists study birds.

You can find out more about genetics on page 34.

Over two million types, or species, of animals and plants have already been identified. Some explorers are biologists too, and new species are still being discovered.

Subjects such as medicine and agriculture are also forms of biology. The research biologists do can provide information on how to improve farming methods and breed healthier animals and crops.

The main interest of many biologists today involves studying things that are too small to be seen without a microscope. This includes learning about microscopic organisms, such as bacteria, and about subjects such as genetics*.

Biologists are also concerned about pollution and how to look after our surroundings.

What do biologists do?

Biologists try to understand as much as possible about the bodies of animals and plants, and how they work. Each part of a living organism has a special job to do. It may help it move, feed or reproduce, or help it survive in a particular climate or surroundings. A biologist looks at the structures of animals and plants, and tries to work out reasons why they are the way they are. Here are a few of the questions that a biologist might ask. The answers to most of these have been found, but many others remain a mystery.

How biology began

Many of the earliest biologists were really explorers with an interest in nature. They were usually wealthy men who went abroad and brought back specimens of animals and plants to study.

Biology did not really become organized as a science until the 18th century. Then Karl von Linne (or Linnaeus, as he is often called), a Swedish botanist, worked out a method for grouping and naming living organisms. Each animal and plant was given a name in Latin, which was the international language of scholars at that time. This system of classification* is used today by biologists all over the world.

Why do the leaves of a Swiss Cheese Plant have holes in them?

Swiss Cheese Plants grow naturally in rocky places, which are exposed to wind. The holes may help protect the leaves from strong wind. Or they may allow light to pass through to leaves lower down the stem**.

Why does this insect look like a stick?

Many animals, like this stick insect, are coloured or shaped so that they blend in with their surroundings. This is called camouflage. It prevents them from being seen and eaten by other animals.

Why does this flower look like an insect?

Many flowers need insects to help them reproduce. They have various ways of attracting the insects. The flowers of this orchid look like the female of a certain species of bee. The male bees are fooled into thinking that the flowers are female bees.

4

*You can find out more about classification on page 36.
**You can find out why light is important to plants on page 10.

Why do roses and hedgehogs have thorns and prickles?

Animals and plants have prickles or stings in order to defend themselves. It's another way to avoid being eaten. Roses also use their thorns for scrambling over other plants, to reach light.

Why does the camel have a hump?

Camels live in deserts, where food and water are usually scarce. The camel has a store of food in its hump, which is made of fat. This keeps it going for several days without food.

Why have some animals and plants died out?

Dinosaur

Dodo

Great Auk

Some animals and plants are much better adapted for survival than others. Over the centuries, many of the less well-adapted species have died out.

Being a biologist

Like all scientists, a biologist has to work rather like a detective. This involves asking questions, then trying to work out the answers. A biologist works from a hunch, called a hypothesis. The hypothesis is then tested with experiments and observations.

With most biology experiments, it is important to do a "control". A control is an experiment that is the same as the experiment you are doing, except for one factor. All the other conditions must be exactly the same. This enables you to be sure whether or not the factor is influencing the result. There is advice on how to do controls with the experiments in this book.

If you're handling chemicals, remember to wash your hands after experiments. Never taste chemicals, or touch your eyes while doing an experiment.

A magnifying glass or microscope will be very useful to help you see things in more detail. You can find out about using microscopes on page 43.

Biologists often use cutaway drawings, like this one, so you can see inside an animal or plant. Many of the colours in this book are not true-to-life, but will help you see details more clearly.

You will find puzzles and questions as you read through the book. The answers to these are at the back.

What living things have in common

Animals and plants are more alike than you might think. They all carry out certain functions which are common to all living things. One of the jobs of a biologist is to find out how each animal and plant is adapted to carry out these functions. From page 10 onwards, you can find out about them in more detail.

1 Food

All living things need food, just as cars need fuel. Food gives them energy for the activities going on inside their bodies. Plants make their own food from sunlight, water and a gas in the air called carbon dioxide. Animals get their food by eating plants or other animals.

Sun

Carbon dioxide

2 Respiration

In order to get energy from food, animals and plants carry out a process called respiration. In most cases, this involves taking in oxygen and giving out carbon dioxide. Plants exchange these gases through tiny holes in their leaves. Animals can take in oxygen in a variety of ways. For instance, fish can absorb oxygen from water through their gills.

3 Waste

Respiration and feeding also produce waste substances which the animal or plant does not need. Getting rid of them is called excretion. Plants excrete through their leaves. Humans do it in various ways, such as sweating, breathing out and going to the toilet.

*You can buy this at the chemist's.

Breathing test

You can do a test to show that you breathe out carbon dioxide. Put some limewater* in a jar. Limewater is a clear liquid which goes milky if you mix it with carbon dioxide. Blow into the jar with a straw. What happens?

Use sprouting seeds, such as mung beans (bean shoots).

Keep the lid on during the experiment.

Put them in a piece of loose-woven material, such as gauze or muslin.

Limewater

You can do a similar test with plants, though it may take a few days before you get a reaction.

4 Sensitivity

Have you ever noticed that crocuses only open their petals when the sun is shining? All living things are sensitive to changes in their surroundings, though some are more sensitive than others. Mammals have a wide range of senses. For instance, a zebra can use its sight, hearing and smell to sense a lion approaching.

5 Movement

All living things move, even though plants usually move too slowly for you to see. If you leave a potted plant by a window for a few days, you may find that the leaves have turned towards the window. Most animals can move their whole bodies, whereas plants can only move parts of them. Moving your whole body, so that you can get from place to place, is called locomotion.

6 Growth

All living things grow. Some organisms, such as trees, keep on growing throughout their lives. Others, like us, reach a certain size and then stop. Some organisms, such as plants, do most of their growing at certain times of year.

7 Reproduction

Nothing lives forever, so it is important that all living things should be able to produce offspring, or new versions of themselves. This is called reproduction.

Microscopic organisms, such as this paramecium, can reproduce simply by dividing in two. This is called asexual reproduction, which means that the new organism is produced from only one parent.

Most animals and plants reproduce sexually, from two parents. A new animal or plant is produced when a male sex cell joins a female sex cell, in a process called fertilization. The male sex cells in flowering plants are contained in a powder called pollen. Insects often help carry pollen to the female sex cells of other plants.

Why isn't a car a living thing?

In many ways a car is just like a living thing. It needs food (petrol) and it excretes waste (from the exhaust pipe). It turns the food into energy in the combustion chambers. It moves and it is sensitive to the touch of the hand on the steering wheel. So why isn't it alive?

What are living things made of?

All living organisms are made up of tiny things called cells, each containing lots of different parts. Your body has about 50 billion cells; some microscopic organisms only have one. Cells were first discovered in the 17th century, by an English scientist, Robert Hooke. Most cells can only be seen with a very powerful microscope*, but you can see some with an ordinary one. There are many kinds of cells, but they all have the same basic features. Try to imagine a cell as a sort of factory. Each part has a special job to do.

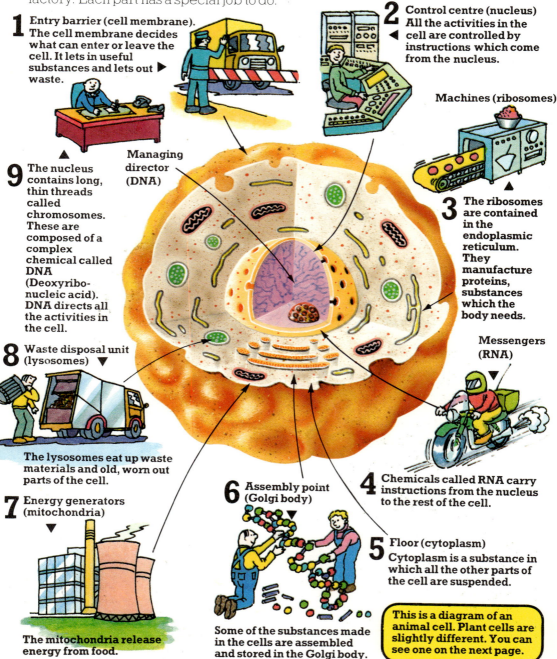

1 **Entry barrier (cell membrane).** The cell membrane decides what can enter or leave the cell. It lets in useful substances and lets out ▶ waste.

2 **Control centre (nucleus)** All the activities in the cell are controlled by instructions which come from the nucleus.

Machines (ribosomes)

3 The ribosomes are contained in the endoplasmic reticulum. They manufacture proteins, substances which the body needs.

Managing director (DNA)

9 The nucleus contains long, thin threads called chromosomes. These are composed of a complex chemical called DNA (Deoxyribonucleic acid). DNA directs all the activities in the cell.

Messengers (RNA)

8 **Waste disposal unit (lysosomes)** ▼

The lysosomes eat up waste materials and old, worn out parts of the cell.

4 Chemicals called RNA carry instructions from the nucleus to the rest of the cell.

7 **Energy generators (mitochondria)** ▼

The mitochondria release energy from food.

6 **Assembly point (Golgi body)** ▼

Some of the substances made in the cells are assembled and stored in the Golgi body.

5 **Floor (cytoplasm)** Cytoplasm is a substance in which all the other parts of the cell are suspended.

This is a diagram of an animal cell. Plant cells are slightly different. You can see one on the next page.

*See page 46 to find out about looking at cells with a microscope.

Plant cells

Plant cells are larger than animal cells, and are often oblong in shape. They have a few extra features that animal cells do not have. Here is a diagram of a plant cell.

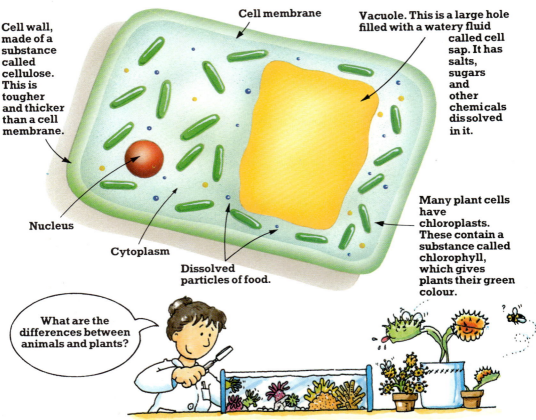

Cell membrane

Vacuole. This is a large hole filled with a watery fluid called cell sap. It has salts, sugars and other chemicals dissolved in it.

Cell wall, made of a substance called cellulose. This is tougher and thicker than a cell membrane.

Nucleus

Cytoplasm

Dissolved particles of food.

Many plant cells have chloroplasts. These contain a substance called chlorophyll, which gives plants their green colour.

What are the differences between animals and plants?

The differences between animals and plants are not always as obvious as it might seem. There are plants that eat animals, and animals, such as corals and sea anemones, that look rather like plants. In the case of some microscopic organisms, biologists often disagree about which category they belong to. Here is a general guide to the differences between them.

Differences between animals and plants

*Animals take in food, by means of a mouth, or similar organ. Plants make their own food from sunlight, carbon dioxide and water.

*Most animals are capable of locomotion; most plants are not.

*Animals are more sensitive than plants. Plants only respond slowly to changes around them.

*Most plants contain chlorophyll and cellulose. No animal contains these.

Animal and plant puzzles

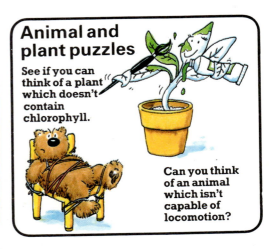

See if you can think of a plant which doesn't contain chlorophyll.

Can you think of an animal which isn't capable of locomotion?

9

Making food

All living organisms need food, to provide energy for the cells to carry out their activities, and for growth and repair. Plants are able to make food, by capturing some of the Sun's energy. They do this in a process called photosynthesis, which means "making things with light". Plants are the only organisms capable of doing this. All animals depend on them – directly or indirectly – for their food.

Solar panels

We can use the Sun's energy too, but not for making food. Solar panels convert it into electrical energy, which can be used to help run a spaceship or for heating houses.

How plants make food

To make food, plants need sunlight, chlorophyll, carbon dioxide and water. The leaves are a plant's main food factories. The chlorophyll contained in many of their cells is used to trap sunlight.

Carbon dioxide　　**Sunlight**

1 Carbon dioxide from the air enters the leaves through tiny pores called stomata.

2 Water from the soil is absorbed through the roots. It then travels up tiny tubes in the stem and then branches off to form a network of tiny veins. You can see these veins if you look very closely at a leaf.

3 Sunlight energy is absorbed by chlorophyll.

4 A chemical reaction takes place in the leaves. The chlorophyll uses the Sun's energy to manufacture glucose (a kind of sugar) from the water and carbon dioxide. In many plants this is then converted to starch.

Chlorophyll making glucose

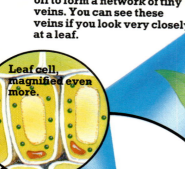

Leaf cell, magnified even more.

Cross-section of a leaf, magnified to about 30 times its real size.

Stomata

Water

Leaves are usually thin and flat, so that as much chlorophyll as possible is exposed to the light.

Plants make other kinds of food too. To do this they need minerals, such as nitrates and phosphates, which are found in the soil. These are dissolved in water and absorbed through a plant's roots.

All plants, except fungi, contain chlorophyll, but they don't all look green. Seaweeds have different coloured pigments such as brown and red masking the chlorophyll. Some parts of the sea get very little light, and these different coloured pigments help the seaweed to absorb whatever light is available.

Green seaweed at the top

Brown seaweed in the middle

Red seaweed at the bottom

Starch experiment

Here is an experiment you can do to prove that plants need light and chlorophyll to make starch. Choose a variegated plant, such as a geranium, which has green and non-green parts on its leaves.

1 Leave the plant in a dark cupboard for a couple of days. This stops it carrying out photosynthesis, so it has to use up its supplies of starch.

2 To make sure there is no starch left, plunge a leaf in boiling water for a few seconds. Then turn off the heat and put the leaf in a jar with some methylated spirits. Put the jar inside the pan of boiling water, to make it boil. This should remove the colour.

Tweezers

Methylated spirits

Be careful! Make sure the cooker is switched off when you're using methylated spirits.

3 Wash the leaf and add a few drops of iodine solution*. If the leaf goes blue-black, it contains starch, so you need to leave the plant a bit longer. If it goes brown, there is no starch left.

Dropper

Iodine solution

4 Attach a piece of black paper to both sides of a leaf on the plant. Leave it in a sunny place for a day. Draw a diagram of the leaf.

Paper clip

Black paper

5 After a day, remove the leaf and test for starch. The results should correspond with your diagram. Only the green parts which were left uncovered should contain starch.

Diagram of leaf

Result of starch test

Not all plants make starch from glucose. You could try this experiment on a variety of plants to find out which ones do.

*You can buy this at a chemist's.

Feeding

As animals cannot make their own food, they get theirs by eating plants, or animals that have eaten plants. In doing so, energy passes from the plant to the animal that eats it, and so on. Biologists call this an energy flow, or a food chain. Here you can see an example of a food chain. With each link in the chain, the amount of energy transferred gets smaller. This is because some of it has already been used up by the animal or plant in carrying out its activities.

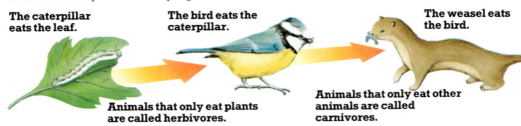

The caterpillar eats the leaf.

The bird eats the caterpillar.

The weasel eats the bird.

Animals that only eat plants are called herbivores.

Animals that only eat other animals are called carnivores.

Food chains are often more complicated than this, because many animals eat a variety of things. When a food chain has several different branches, biologists call it a food web.

Animals, like us, that eat plants and animals are called omnivores.

Herbivores and carnivores

Herbivores and carnivores have features to suit their different eating habits. Carnivores need good long-distance eyesight, in order to spot their prey, and they have to be able to move quickly and quietly to catch it. Herbivores need to be able to see animals approaching from all directions, so that they can avoid being eaten. For instance, look at the differences between a cat and a mouse.

Pair of forward-pointing eyes, which help it judge distances accurately.

Camouflaged colouring to help it hide easily.

Sensitive ears help it detect the approach of an enemy.

Large, light-sensitive eyes. These help it see in dark places, such as tunnels, where it can hide from enemies.

Eyes to the sides of the head. This gives it good all-round sight.

Soft-padded feet, to enable it to move quietly.

Sharp claws to capture food.

Mobile fingers, to help it hold awkward food, such as nuts.

Eyesight test

Animals with eyes to the sides of their heads can't judge distances very accurately. This is because the pictures they form with each eye don't overlap very much. Animals like us, with eyes at the front of their heads, have binocular vision. This means that they use both eyes together. Try holding a pencil almost at arm's length. Then, with one eye closed, try to touch the top very quickly with one of your fingers. Then try it with both eyes. Which is more accurate?

How food is recycled

When animals and plants die, their bodies rot and eventually disappear into the soil. Rotting is caused by organisms, such as bacteria or fungi, which are known as decomposers. Decomposers feed on the dead bodies of animals and plants. They break them down into simple raw materials and release nitrates and other substances into the soil. These are absorbed by plants and used to help them make food.

Plants

The blue arrows show energy used up by the animal or plant for its own activities.

Carnivores

Decomposers

Herbivores

Carnivores

The orange arrows show energy passed along the food chain.

The purple arrows show all parts of the food chain returning to the soil, to be used again by plants.

Mouths

Animals feed in a variety of different ways. Their mouths are adapted for the kind of food they eat.

Butterflies and moths feed on nectar in flowers. They have a long, coiled tube called a proboscis, which uncoils to reach inside the flower. ▼

◀ **Insect-eating birds often have long, pointed beaks, to help them look for food inside cracks in trees.**

Seed-eating birds tend to have short, blunt beaks to pick up the seeds. ◀

Snails eat grass, leaves and flowers. A snail has a rough-edged tongue, rather like a file, which can saw off bits of vegetation.
▼

Monkey puzzle

Why do you think animals that live in trees have forward-pointing eyes?

Carnivorous plants

Some plants live in soils which are poor in nitrates. They can make up for this by catching insects and other animals, whose bodies contain the chemicals they need. The Venus Fly-Trap catches flies and absorbs them into its body.

What happens to food

Food contains many different, useful substances, such as proteins, carbohydrates and fats. But in order for the body to make use of them, the food has to get inside the cells. The food you eat wouldn't fit into tiny cells, so it has to go through several processes first. It is chewed with the teeth, and then digested, or broken down, into smaller, simpler chemicals. These chemicals dissolve in the blood, which carries them round the body to the cells.

Teeth

Mammals' teeth come in different shapes and sizes, to suit their different eating habits.

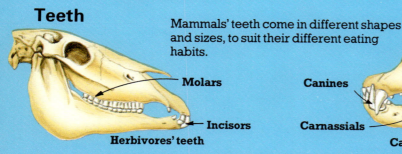

Molars

Incisors

Herbivores' teeth

Canines

Carnassials

Carnivores' teeth

Plants contain a lot of "woody" material that is difficult to digest, so herbivores have to chew their food a lot before swallowing it. Herbivores have flat, ridged teeth, called molars, to grind their food and sharp front teeth, called incisors, to cut it. Carnivores have long, pointed teeth, called canines, for ripping up raw flesh. Their back teeth, or carnassials, are for slicing meat into small pieces. Humans have canines, molars and incisors too, but the differences between them are not as pronounced as in other animals. This is because we eat a lot of different things.

Jaws

The jaws of herbivores and carnivores vary too. Dogs move their jaws up and down to crush their food. Horses and cows move their jaws round and round in a circular grinding motion.

What food is used for

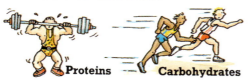

Proteins

Carbohydrates

Fats

Vitamins and minerals

*Proteins give you energy and build you up. They enable you to grow, and to replace dead cells as they wear away. The main protein foods are meat, fish, eggs, milk and vegetables like lentils.
*Carbohydrates are the main energy-giving foods. You find carbohydrates in starchy foods, such as bread, potatoes, yams, rice and pasta, and in sugary foods, such as sweets and cakes.

*Fats give energy too, and can provide a store of food beneath your skin and help keep you warm. Fats are found in milk, butter, cream, cheese and meat.
*Many foods also contain vitamins and minerals. You only need small quantities of these, but they are very important for keeping different parts of the body in good condition.

Digestion

Once you've swallowed your food, it begins a long journey which ends in the cells. Digestion starts in the mouth and continues in the gut, or alimentary canal. This is a tube about 7m long, which stretches from the mouth to the anus. Food is broken down by digestive juices, which contain important chemicals called enzymes. All animals have some kind of digestive system. Here you can find out about the human digestive system.

What do enzymes do?

Enzymes help speed up digestion. Without them the process would take much longer. Carbohydrates are broken down into sugars, such as glucose. Proteins are broken down into amino acids. Fats are broken down into glycerol and fatty acids.

Enzymes

Saliva experiment

Saliva contains an enzyme which digests starch. Try chewing a piece of bread for a few minutes without swallowing it. It will start to taste sweet, which shows that the starch has been turned into a sugar.

Jelly and pineapple experiment

Pineapple contains an enzyme which digests protein. You could try this experiment to show how it does this. Jelly contains a protein called gelatine. Make two small jellies, one with fresh pineapple and one with tinned pineapple. The one with fresh pineapple won't set properly, because the enzyme breaks down the gelatine. Enzymes only work at certain temperatures. Tinned pineapple has been boiled first, which destroys the enzyme. So the jelly with tinned pineapple should set properly.

In the mouth, the food is chewed and mixed with saliva. This moistens it and makes it easier to swallow.

As you swallow, your tongue pushes food into your throat and down the oesophagus.

Mouth

Food is squeezed along the gut by two layers of muscles contracting alternately. This is called peristalsis.

The stomach stores food and controls its flow to the rest of the gut. It releases digestive juices and an acid, which helps kill any bacteria.

Oesophagus

One of the liver's jobs is to make a green liquid called bile, which helps break up fats.

Liver

Stomach

Pancreas

Large intestine

Digestive juices are released into the duodenum from the pancreas. These contain enzymes which can digest all types of food.

Duodenum

Ileum

Digestion is completed in the ileum. The wall of the ileum contains lots of finger-like structures called villi. The walls of the villi are only one cell thick. Digested food can pass through them and into tiny blood vessels on the other side.

Anus

Some of the things you eat, known as roughage, cannot be digested. They pass along the large intestine to the anus, where they are eliminated from the body.

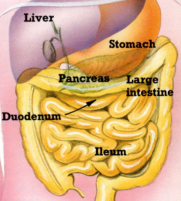

15

Getting energy

Food alone cannot provide energy for living organisms to use. The energy has to be released from the food in a chemical reaction called respiration. Food is rather like a fuel, such as coal. Coal is a source of energy which can be used to drive machinery and keep us warm. But it can't do this on its own. Before it can give off energy, it has to be combined with oxygen from the air and burned. It is the same with food. In order to release energy from food, most organisms have to combine it with oxygen. They give off carbon dioxide as a waste product. This is why you need to breathe.

How the energy is used

Your body uses energy in various ways. It powers your muscles, so you can move. It helps you grow and gives your cells energy, so they can carry out their activities. Some energy is released as heat, which keeps your body warm. In some animals, it is released as light or electricity.

Firefly

Glow-worm

Electric eel

Keeping the gases circulating

Green plants help to keep the gases in the air balanced. They take in oxygen and give out carbon dioxide just as animals do. But during photosynthesis, they take in even larger quantities of carbon dioxide and give out large amounts of oxygen as waste. Without plants, the supply of oxygen in the air would eventually run out.

Oxygen

Carbon dioxide

*See page 10.

How living things respire

In order to carry out respiration, most animals and plants need to take in oxygen and give out carbon dioxide. Biologists call this "exchanging gases". Plants do it through the stomata* in their leaves. Many animals exchange gases by breathing. Oxygen is taken in through the nose or mouth and into the windpipe and lungs, where it passes into the bloodstream. Here a pair of lungs has been cut away so you can see inside.

Bronchi (pronounced brong-kee)

Bronchioles

The windpipe divides into two main passages called bronchi. These split up into hundreds of tiny tubes, called bronchioles, rather like the branches of a tree.

Why do you pant after exercise?

What is aerobics?

Respiration which uses oxygen is called "aerobic" respiration. Aerobics is the name given to exercise which increases the flow of oxygen around the body. It is hard, but not exhausting, and can be kept up for a long time. Exercise such as sprinting is "anaerobic", because you have to produce a lot of energy too fast for your body to cope aerobically. You can respire anaerobically for a short time. Too much anaerobic respiration produces lactic acid in your muscles, which makes them ache and gives you cramp.

What happens when you breathe?

When you breathe in, tiny air sacs, called alveoli, fill with air. Oxygen in the air passes through the walls of the alveoli into tiny blood vessels. The blood carries the oxygen to the cells, where it is exchanged for waste carbon dioxide. Carbon dioxide is carried back to the lungs and breathed out.

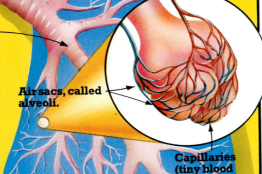

Air sacs, called alveoli.

Capillaries (tiny blood vessels)

You could try to work out how much air your lungs will hold. Take a deep breath and blow into a large plastic bag.

Energy experiment

You could try this experiment to show that plants, as well as animals, give off energy in respiration. You can test this by finding out whether they produce heat. Use sprouting seeds, such as mung beans (bean sprouts)*.

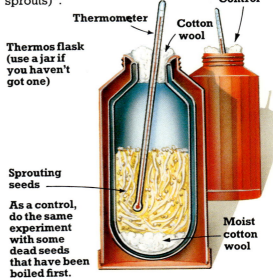

Thermometer

Cotton wool

Control

Thermos flask (use a jar if you haven't got one)

Sprouting seeds

As a control, do the same experiment with some dead seeds that have been boiled first.

Moist cotton wool

After a few days, read the two thermometers. You should find that the temperature of the one containing the live seeds is higher than the other one.

How other animals exchange gases

All gas exchange systems have certain things in common. They need to be moist and in close contact with the air and blood (or other circulation system), so that oxygen can get to the cells.

Birds have a very efficient breathing system, with lungs that extend even into some bones. Birds appear to breathe as they beat their wings – about 200 times a minute.

 An insect's gas exchange system consists of a series of tubes running through its body, with tiny pores opening on to the outside.

 Fish absorb oxygen from water through their gills, which contain tiny capillaries.

 Frogs can breathe in several ways, including through their moist skin.

Anaerobes

Some organisms, known as anaerobes, can respire anaerobically all the time. They often live deep in the soil, where there is little oxygen. Yeast is partly an anaerobe. Wine is made by yeast carrying out anaerobic respiration. The yeast feeds on grape juice and gives off carbon dioxide, without using oxygen.

Chickens respire aerobically with their leg muscles.

They respire anaerobically during take-off with their breast muscle.

*You can get these from a health food or garden shop.

How substances move around the body

All living things need some method of moving substances around their bodies. Food and oxygen have to be taken to the cells, and waste, such as carbon dioxide, has to be taken away from them. In plants, food and water are carried by bundles of tubes called the phloem and xylem. In animals, food and other substances are carried by the blood. Biologists refer to these as transport systems.

What does blood do?

Blood does a number of different jobs. It carries substances to and from the cells, it eats up germs and helps repair wounds by clotting. Blood is made up of a liquid called plasma, which contains blood cells and dissolved particles of food and waste. There are three main types of blood cells.

Red blood cells carry the oxygen. They contain a red pigment, or colouring, called haemoglobin. Red blood cells wear out and are replaced about every four months.

White blood cells are larger, but not nearly as numerous as red ones. Their main job is to eat up bacteria and fight infections. They only last a few days.

Platelets are tiny fragments of cells, which help the blood to clot when you cut yourself.

How blood gets around the bod

Blood circulates the body in tubes, called blood vessels. This process is kept going by the heart, which is a pump made of muscle. There are three types of blood vessels. Vessels which carry blood to the heart are called veins. They have valves to

How circulation works

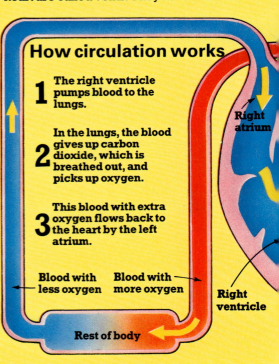

1 The right ventricle pumps blood to the lungs.

2 In the lungs, the blood gives up carbon dioxide, which is breathed out, and picks up oxygen.

3 This blood with extra oxygen flows back to the heart by the left atrium.

Blood with less oxygen

Blood with more oxygen

Right atrium

Right ventricle

Rest of body

What is a heartbeat?

A heartbeat is the sound made by the heart valves closing. The heart usually beats about 70 times a minute. You can hear it if you put your ear to someone's chest. You can get an even louder sound if you use a microphone and put the sound through an amplifier onto a tape.

Test your pulse

Every time your heart beats, there is a rush of blood along the arteries, away from the heart. You can feel this as a sort of throb, called a pulse, on your wrist. Press lightly with one or two fingers on the largest artery. It is not always easy to find the right place, so you may have to try several times. Time it to see how many beats there are in a minute. Try again after exercise, such as running. How much difference is there?

Did you know?

You have so many capillaries in your body that they would stretch round the world twice, if you laid them end to end.

ensure that the blood flows in the right direction. Vessels which carry blood away from the heart are called arteries. Capillaries are narrow, thin-walled vessels, through which substances such as food and oxygen can pass into the blood.

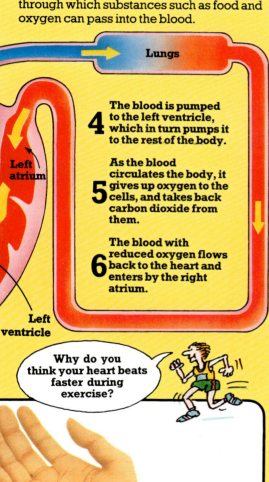

Lungs

4 The blood is pumped to the left ventricle, which in turn pumps it to the rest of the body.

5 As the blood circulates the body, it gives up oxygen to the cells, and takes back carbon dioxide from them.

6 The blood with reduced oxygen flows back to the heart and enters by the right atrium.

Left atrium

Left ventricle

Why do you think your heart beats faster during exercise?

How do substances get in and out of cells?

Carbon dioxide diffusing out

Oxygen diffusing in

The cell membrane decides which substances may enter or leave a cell. There are several methods by which it does this, not all of which are fully understood by biologists. Many simple substances, such as oxygen, pass through by a method known as diffusion.

Particles diffusing across cell membrane

Equal concentration of particles

Diffusion happens when there are more particles of certain substances in one area than in another. Some of those particles then move across, so that there is an equal concentration of them everywhere. The diffusion of water is known as osmosis.

Potato chip experiment

You could watch osmosis at work with uncooked potato chips. Put some in a bowl of very salty water. As a control, leave some others in a bowl of ordinary water. After about an hour, the ones in salty water should be limp. Potato cells contain a lot of water. The solution of salt water is more concentrated than the solution inside the cells. So water passes into it from the potato cells, making the potatoes limp. This is why you shouldn't put too much plant food in the water when you're watering your plants.

Plant transport systems

The transport system in plants consists of bundles of tubes in the stem and branches. These tubes are called the phloem (pronounced flo-em) and xylem (pronounced zy-lem). The phloem vessels carry the food manufactured in the leaves to all parts of the plant. The xylem vessels carry water and dissolved minerals from the roots to the rest of the plant.

Water is constantly travelling through a plant. It is taken in through the roots by osmosis and evaporates from the leaves in a process called transpiration. Transpiration cools the leaves and protects them from the Sun. It also causes a kind of suction, which pulls water up the stem from the roots.

Water evaporates from the leaves into the air.

Water sucked up the stem or trunk.

Controlling water loss

Plants lose more water from their leaves when it's hot or very windy. They lose less when it's still or humid. To keep healthy, plants need to maintain a steady water content. So many plants are adapted to prevent them losing too much water.

Phloem and xylem

Here you can see a slice through the stem, showing the phloem and xylem vessels.

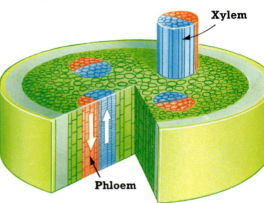

Xylem

Phloem

Why do you think cacti have spines as leaves?

Why do you think trees lose their leaves in winter?

Plants and water

You could try this experiment to show water being sucked up a stem. Put some water and food colouring into a jar with a cut plant. Choose one with a transparent stem, such as celery, so you can see inside. Leave the plant for a few hours.

Water has been sucked up to here.

You will be able to see from the dye how far the water has travelled up the stem. If the plant doesn't have a transparent stem, cut slices off so you can see inside.

Another way to show that water is taken up by the plant is to mark the water level on the jar when you begin. Cover the water with oil, to stop it evaporating.

Coloured dye and water

Which side of a leaf loses most water?

To find the answer, tape a piece of cobalt chloride paper* to both sides of a leaf. As it comes in contact with water, the paper will turn pink. Which side goes pink first?

Cobalt chloride paper

Water absorbed by the roots.

*You can buy cobalt chloride paper at most chemist's.

Waste disposal

All animals need to keep the substances inside their bodies at a safe level. This is called homeostasis. This involves regulating the supply of substances, such as glucose and oxygen, in the blood, and getting rid of waste, or excretion. In mammals this is carried out by the lungs (which excrete carbon dioxide), the skin (which removes excess heat), the liver and kidneys. These are called the excretory organs.

What the liver does

The liver contains hundreds of enzymes*, which help it do a variety of jobs. Any food not immediately needed by the cells is taken to the liver and stored. Excess proteins are broken down to release urea, a waste product which is taken to the kidneys and excreted in urine. The liver also removes poisons, such as alcohol and medicines. This is why you have to take medicines at regular intervals – because the liver keeps on removing them. All these activities produce heat, which is spread around the body in the blood.

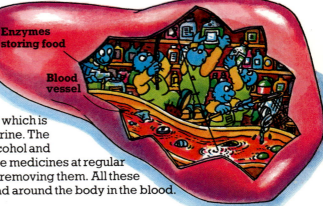

Enzymes storing food

Blood vessel

Liver enzyme experiment

You could try this experiment to see a liver enzyme at work. Many cells produce a waste product called hydrogen peroxide. Liver contains an enzyme called catalase, which breaks this down into water and oxygen.

Put some diluted hydrogen peroxide ** in a jar with a piece of uncooked liver.**

If catalase is present, you should see bubbles of oxygen gas given off. The control may give off bubbles too, but there should be much fewer.

Control

Be careful! Keep hydrogen peroxide away from your skin and eyes.

Bubbles of gas

Liver

Hydrogen peroxide

As a control, put some hydrogen peroxide in another jar, without liver.

Other animals and plants contain catalase. You could try the same experiment with celery or potato.

What the kidneys do

The kidneys are the main excretory organs. Each one contains over a million microscopic filtering units, called nephrons. The kidneys filter the blood, removing urea, excess salts and water. Together these form a liquid called urine, which travels along two tubes, called ureters, to the bladder. The bladder empties when you go to the toilet. The kidneys control the amount of water in your body. The more you drink, the more urine you produce.

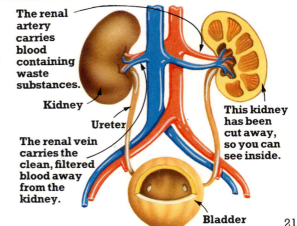

The renal artery carries blood containing waste substances.

Kidney

Ureter

The renal vein carries the clean, filtered blood away from the kidney.

This kidney has been cut away, so you can see inside.

Bladder

21

*Enzymes are chemicals which speed up reactions in the body.
**You can buy hydrogen peroxide at the chemist's.

Skeletons and movement

All animals and plants need some means of supporting their bodies. Otherwise they would lose shape and collapse. A skeleton is one kind of support. It provides an animal with a rigid frame, which gives it shape and enables it to move. All animals need to be able to move – to find food, or a mate, or to defend themselves from attack. Plants move too, though their movements are more limited*.

Jellyfish   **Seaweed**

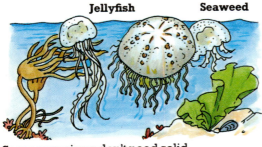

Some organisms don't need solid skeletons. Sea creatures, such as jellyfish and seaweed are supported by fluid inside their bodies, and by the water itself. Seaweed is much too limp to stand up by itself on land.

You can support yourself quite easily in water too. Try supporting the weight of your whole body on a couple of fingers.

Many plants, and a few animals such as caterpillars, are also supported by the pressure of water inside their cells. This is why a plant flops over if it doesn't get enough water. Mature trees are supported by the wood in their stems.

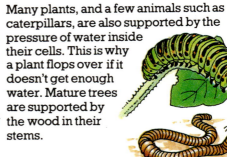

External skeletons

Beetle

Some animals, such as insects and crabs, have an external skeleton, called an exoskeleton. It is rather like a suit of armour, made up of hard plates and tubes with moveable joints.

Moving in the air

To fly, an animal needs to be light, to have something to push against the air, and a shape which will keep it there.

Birds have very light, hollow bones and powerful muscles attached to their wings.

How lift works

The shape of a bird's wing forces air to move more quickly across the top of it than underneath it. Try blowing between two short strips of paper (about 2cm by 5cm), one just above the other. The lower one should rise to meet the upper one as the two are sucked together. This is similar to what happens in "lift".

Birds' wings are light and have a large surface area. Their shape provides a force called a lift, which helps the bird stay in the air.

These are called contour feathers. They work like tiles, covering the base of the wing, giving it a smooth, streamlined shape.

These are called flight feathers. They are hollow and light and are made up of hundreds of tiny hooks, which hold the feather together.

*You can find out about plant movement on page 24.

Internal skeletons

Mammals, birds, fish, reptiles and amphibians all have an internal skeleton made up of bones and cartilage, or gristle.

Bones are held together at joints, by fibres called ligaments. The joints are kept well oiled by a lubricating fluid, called synovial fluid. There are several kinds of joints.

The neck contains a pivot joint. This allows you to swivel your head from side to side.

Did you know?

A giraffe has the same number of bones in its neck as a human.

Knees, elbows and fingers are hinge joints. They move backwards and forwards like a door.

The hip is a ball and socket joint. It enables you to move your leg in practically any direction.

What are bones made of?

You could get a bone from the butcher's to investigate. Bones contain a mixture of chemicals, including large amounts of calcium and protein. To remove the protein, heat a small piece in a very hot flame* for about 10 minutes. This makes it hard, white and brittle. To remove calcium, leave another bone in dilute hydrochloric acid** for a few days. This makes it bendy and rubbery. Calcium or protein on its own would be unsuitable for a skeleton. But together they make it both strong and flexible.

Moving in water

Water is much denser, or heavier, than air. This is why walking in water is slower than walking on land. Fish, however, are specially adapted for moving in water. The fastest fish can move almost as fast as a cheetah.

A fish contains a swim-bladder, an air-filled space, which makes it buoyant and stops it sinking.

A fish swims by sweeping its body from side to side. It has powerful muscles on each side of its backbone.

The fins act rather like rudders on a boat.

A fish's body has a streamlined shape.

Muscles

Muscles are attached to the joints by strong, non-stretchy fibres called tendons. They pull against the skeleton and enable it to move. Muscles can pull bones towards them, by contracting, but they cannot push.

*You could put it in a coal fire or bonfire, or hold it with tongs over a gas flame.
**You can buy this at the chemist's.

23

Sensitivity

Sensitivity is essential for survival. All animals and plants are capable of sensing changes in their environment. A change in light, sound, smell, touch or temperature, is known as a stimulus. Most animals have sense organs, such as ears or eyes, which are adapted to receive a particular stimulus. The organs contain sensitive cells, which receive information and pass it to the brain by means of nerves*. Animals are not all sensitive to the same things. Some have a wide range of senses; others rely almost entirely on one sense. Plants don't have distinct sense organs, but certain parts of their bodies are sensitive to particular stimuli.

Light and vision

Most organisms are sensitive to light, but not all are capable of vision. Vision means using eyes to form a picture of the world around you. The eyes take in light rays, which are focussed by a lens on to light-sensitive cells at the back of the eye. The cells send messages to the brain, which interprets them as what you see.

Insects have compound eyes, made up of large numbers of tiny lenses. The picture they see is probably rather blurred. Dragonflies rely almost entirely on sight. They have nearly 30,000 lenses in each eye.

Dragonfly's eyes

Bees can see ultra-violet light, which we cannot see. This enables them to see lines on the petals of flowers, which guides them towards nectar.

Animals that live by night, such as owls, often have big eyes. This helps them take in as much light as is available.

Plants and light

Plants respond to light by growing towards or away from it. (Some prefer shade.) This experiment shows you which part of a plant is sensitive to light.

Grow some wheat, barley or oat seeds in seed compost.

When they are about 10mm high, cover the tips of half of them with silver foil. Leave about 7mm of stem exposed.

Silver foil

Position the box with a bright light to one side of it.

After a few days, the uncovered shoots should have started to bend and grow towards the light. The covered ones should still be straight, showing that it is the tip of the shoot that detects light. The plant does most of its growing just beneath the tip.

What we see

What the bee sees

How flowers respond to light

Some flowers, such as crocuses, only open their petals on sunny days. Others open and close at certain times of day. Some gardeners make flower clocks. The flowers are arranged in a circle, according to the time of day they open or close.

These are called evening primroses, because they don't open until about 6 p.m.

24

You can find out more about nerves on page 26.

Sound, vibration and gravity

Sounds are really vibrations in the air. In mammals, the sense organs for sound are the ears. Your ears also help you keep your balance.

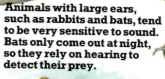

Animals with large ears, such as rabbits and bats, tend to be very sensitive to sound. Bats only come out at night, so they rely on hearing to detect their prey.

Fish don't have ears. They pick up vibrations by means of sensitive cells along a part of the body called the lateral line.

Animals with long whiskers, such as gerbils, are sensitive to vibrations.

Lateral line

Plants are sensitive to gravity. No matter which way you plant a seed, it will grow in the right direction. Try turning a young shoot on its side. Leave it in the dark for a few days and keep it well watered. What happens? ▶

Keep the soil well packed in.

Smell and taste

In mammals, the nose and tongue are the sense organs for smell and taste. Many animals have a much better sense of smell than humans. This helps them search for food and avoid being eaten.

Antennae

Insects, such as moths, smell with their antennae.

Flies taste with their feet. They walk over their food before eating it.

Touch

The skin is the organ for sensing touch, pain and temperature. There are sensitive nerve endings all over your skin. Very sensitive parts, such as the tongue and fingertips, have more nerve endings.

The back has fewer nerves than other parts. Try touching a friend's back with the ends of two pencils, about 2cm apart. Ask how many pencils there are. Sometimes they may feel them as one touch.

Sensitive plants

Some plants are sensitive to touch. If you touch a Mimosa pudica plant, the leaves will close suddenly and the plant will droop. This makes them less easy to eat.

Draw a map of your tongue

Different parts of the tongue can taste different things. To try this experiment, you need solutions of something sweet (sugary water), salty (salty water), sour (vinegar) and bitter (black tea).

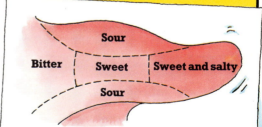

Sour

Bitter | Sweet | Sweet and salty

Sour

Dry your tongue with tissue. Put a drop of one solution on the tip, and then on the sides and back of the tongue. Where can you taste it best? Rinse your mouth and try the other solutions. Make a diagram of the results – it should look something like this.

Co-ordination

All living things need some means of co-ordinating their activities, so that the different parts of their bodies work together as a whole. In most animals, this is achieved by some sort of nervous system. The nervous system in mammals consists of the brain and spinal cord, with bundles of fibres called nerves. Each fibre is part of a nerve cell, called a neurone. Nerves act rather like messengers. It is their job to send messages, in the form of nerve impulses, to and from different parts of the body.

How it works

1 You detect danger with one or more of your sense organs.

2 A nerve impulse is sent to the brain along a sensory nerve.

3 The brain interprets the message and decides what the response should be – in this case, to run.

4 A nerve impulse is sent along a motor nerve to the muscles.

5 The muscles receive the message. They contract, causing your body to move.

All this happens in fractions of a second.

Insect nervous system

An insect's nervous system works in a similar way. Though instead of a brain, it has several organs called ganglia*, the largest of which is in its head. The ganglia receive messages from the sense organs and direct them to other parts of the body.

Large ganglion in head

Ganglia

Nerve cords

Nerves

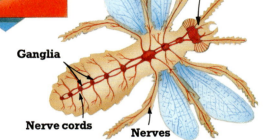

Do you think sneezing or blinking are reflex reactions?

Reflex actions

Many actions, such as kicking a ball, require a conscious decision from the brain. They are called voluntary reactions, because you choose to do them. But there are some actions which are automatic and can by-pass part of the brain. These are called involuntary, or reflex, reactions. Most reflex reactions happen to protect you. For instance, if you touch something hot, your hand will automatically leap away.

26

*The singular is ganglion.

Keeping things under control

In order for the body to work properly, a lot of things have to be kept under control. For instance, the supply of water and the level of the various substances in the blood need to be regulated. Many of these processes, in plants as well as animals, are co-ordinated by chemicals called hormones. In animals, hormones are made by organs called endocrine glands and released into the blood. Hormones do a variety of jobs. For example, if you are excited or in danger, a hormone called adrenalin is produced. Here you can see what it does.

Your muscles generate heat, so you sweat more to get rid of the heat.

To give you more energy, you respire faster. This makes your breathing quicker.

If there is an accident, your blood will clot faster.

Your heart beats faster and blood rushes to your muscles from other parts of the body. This gives you more power if you need to run or fight.

As blood has been diverted away from your skin and stomach, your skin goes pale and you get "butterflies" in the stomach.

Adrenalin makes the cells take up more oxygen and glucose, so they can work faster.

Temperature control

The temperature of the body needs to be kept steady. This is because enzymes, which are vital to many of the body's activities, can only function within a certain range of temperatures. There are various ways of controlling temperature.

When you become too hot, the blood vessels nearest the skin widen, so that more blood passes through them. This makes you look red. Heat from the blood passes through the skin into the air. ▶

◀ Sweat is mainly water and salt. When you get too hot, it comes up through your pores and evaporates. This cools you down.

When you are too cold, your muscles try to compensate by increasing their activity, to create heat. This activity is shivering. ▶

Mammals and birds are called warm-blooded animals, because they can maintain a constant temperature. The activities in their bodies produce heat which they can retain by insulation – with fur, feathers or a layer of fat under the skin.

Penguins have a layer of fat under their skin, which helps them survive in cold climates.

◀ Cold-blooded animals, such as snakes, do not necessarily have cold blood. But they cannot create as much heat inside their bodies. They bask in summer, in order to absorb heat from the Sun.

27

Reproduction

All animals and plants die eventually. So in order for their species to survive, they must be able to reproduce themselves. Most organisms produce offspring from two parents, but some can reproduce from only one.

What is sexual reproduction?

In sexual reproduction, a new animal or plant is formed from two parents. Most animals and all flowering plants reproduce sexually. A male sex cell joins a female sex cell to make a single new cell called a zygote. The zygote divides many times, producing more cells which form the new individual. Sex cells are called gametes and are produced by sex organs. The fusing together of gametes is called fertilization.

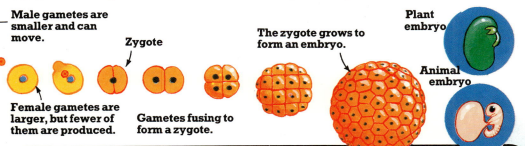

Male gametes are smaller and can move.

Female gametes are larger, but fewer of them are produced.

Zygote

Gametes fusing to form a zygote.

The zygote grows to form an embryo.

Plant embryo

Animal embryo

Plant sex organs

A plant's sex organs are in its flowers. Some plants have male and female organs in the same flower; others have separate male and female flowers. The female sex organs are called carpels. Each carpel contains an ovary and each ovary contains one or more ovules. The female gametes, or eggs, are enclosed in the ovules. The male sex organs are called stamens. Each stamen consists of a stalk with an anther on the end.

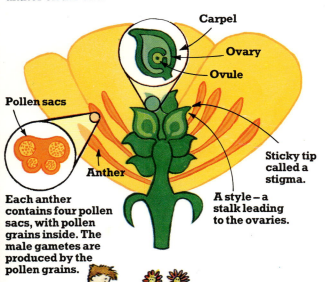

Carpel

Ovary

Ovule

Pollen sacs

Anther

Sticky tip called a stigma.

A style – a stalk leading to the ovaries.

Each anther contains four pollen sacs, with pollen grains inside. The male gametes are produced by the pollen grains.

Animal sex organs

Animals' sex organs all have the same basic features. Here you can see human sex organs. A few animals have both male and female organs.

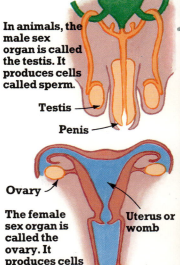

In animals, the male sex organ is called the testis. It produces cells called sperm.

Testis

Penis

Ovary

The female sex organ is called the ovary. It produces cells called ova or eggs.

Uterus or womb

You could try dissecting a large flower, such as a tulip, very carefully with a sharp kitchen knife. Use a magnifying glass to help you identify the different parts.

How fertilization happens

Animals that live in water, such as fish, produce large numbers of eggs and sperm. These are released into the water at the same time. The sperm, which have tails, swim towards the eggs to fertilize them. This is called external fertilization, as it takes place outside the parents' bodies. This method is very risky, as many eggs are eaten and sperm are lost.

Sperm

Eggs

External fertilization would not work on land as the sperm could not swim to meet the eggs. Land animals, including humans, use internal fertilization, which is a more efficient method. The male deposits sperm inside the female's body by means of an organ called a penis.

Some animals, such as frogs, also practise external fertilization, but with a better chance of success. The male clings to the female's back until the eggs are released. Then he releases his sperm so that it pours over the eggs.

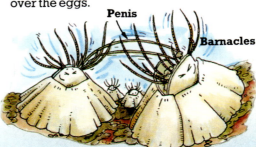

Penis

Barnacles

Pollination

Before fertilization can take place in plants, pollen must be transferred from the anthers to a stigma. This is called pollination. Since flowers cannot move, they rely on one of two methods – animals (usually insects) or wind – to carry the pollen.

Animal-pollinated flowers have brightly coloured, scented petals to attract the animal.

Insects feed on pollen and nectar.

Some flowers are pollinated by other animals, such as birds and bats.

Wind-pollinated flowers do not need to be colourful or scented.

They produce large quantities of pollen, as more tends to get lost.

The male flower has long, protruding anthers, well-exposed to the wind.

The female flowers often have large, feathery stigmas, which make an easy target to hit.

How it happens

The insect visits the flower in search of food. As it does so, it gets brushed with pollen which is picked up by the sticky stigmas of the next flower it visits.

Fertilization

When the pollen lands it sends a tube down the style and into the ovary. Gametes move down the tube to fertilize the egg.

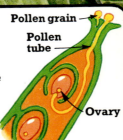

Pollen grain

Pollen tube

Ovary

How the embryo develops

The embryos of frogs and fish develop inside soft eggs in the water. Many of them do not survive as they are often left to develop on their own.

Some land animals, such as birds and reptiles, produce eggs with a hard or leathery shell. This protects the embryo inside and stops it drying up.

Finding somewhere to grow

A plant embryo is contained inside a seed. The seed has a hard, protective wall around it and a store of food inside. Seeds have a better chance of surviving if they grow away from the parent plants. This stops the ground becoming overcrowded. Seeds are designed so that they can be scattered in one of several ways.

The embryos of mammals develop inside the body of the mother. Mammals and birds both look after their offspring. So although they produce relatively small numbers, each one has a better chance of survival.

By animals

The seeds are held by fruits. ▶ Some fruits, such as strawberries and tomatoes, are fleshy and attractive. Animals eat the fruits and the seeds pass through the animals' bodies.

◀ Not all fruits are edible. Some fruits have hooks on them which catch in the fur of passing animals.

By wind

Seeds which are light and ▶ have wings or hairs, such as dandelion seeds, are scattered by the wind.

By explosion

◀ Some seeds develop in pods and are scattered when the pod bursts open.

Which method do you think would take the seed furthest?

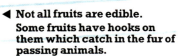

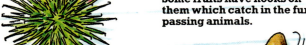

How male seahorses give birth

A female seahorse's eggs are fertilized externally, then deposited in a pouch in the body of the male. As the eggs grow, his body swells in size. The eggs split open inside the pouch, but the young seahorses do not emerge until they are fully developed.

Young seahorse

Asexual reproduction

In asexual reproduction, offspring are produced from one parent only. This method is used mainly by the simplest organisms, such as bacteria, and by plants that don't have flowers. But many flowering plants, and some animals, have asexual as well as sexual methods.

Cell division

One-celled organisms, like this paramecium, reproduce by dividing in two. The nucleus splits and cytoplasm gathers around each one. Paramecia* are found in ponds, but you cannot see them without a microscope.

Spores

Many non-flowering plants, such as fungi, produce tiny cells called spores. These are scattered by rain, wind or insects, and develop into a new individual. If you see a mature puff ball, you could try dropping water on it. It may shed its spores.

Some bacteria can divide as often as once every 20 minutes. Can you work out how many bacteria could be produced from one in 10 hours?

Budding

Hydras are tiny animals, about 2cm long, that live in ponds and slow-moving streams. They can reproduce by budding – growing a new animal on the sides of their bodies.

Asexual reproduction in flowering plants

All flowering plants reproduce sexually by means of seeds, but many of them have asexual methods too.

Runners ▶

Some plants, such as spider plants, put down runners. These are long side shoots which touch the ground and develop roots of their own.

Parent plant

New plants

Runners

◀ Tubers

A potato is a swollen stem, called a tuber. It develops from shoots of a potato plant, which grow into the soil instead of producing branches. Food is stored in the tuber. In winter the plant dies, but the tubers develop into new plants in the following year.

Potato plant

Potato tubers

Bulbs ▶

A bulb is a bud whose leaves are swollen with food. It stays alive over winter when the rest of the plant has died. Sometimes the bulb reproduces asexually, by sprouting an extra bulb to one side.

New bulb

Main bulb

Single parents

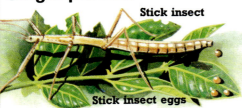

Stick insect

Stick insect eggs ▼

Nearly all stick insects are females. So they produce young from eggs which have not been fertilized. This is called parthenogenesis, which comes from the Greek, meaning "virgin births". Other insects, such as aphids (greenfly), also reproduce by parthenogenesis.

*Plural of paramecium.

31

Life cycles and growth

Most animals and plants begin life as a single cell. The cell divides many times, adding to itself new cells, and so the organism increases in size. As it does so, its structure becomes more complicated, and it develops specialized cells for particular jobs. Some organisms, such as trees, go on growing all their lives. Others, like us, reach a certain size and then stop. The changes that an organism undergoes in the course of its life is known as its life cycle.

Investigating seeds

The life cycle of a plant starts with a seed. You could try investigating the structure of a seed. Soak some large seeds, such as broad bean seeds, in water overnight. The water makes them swell and easy to split open. You should be able to see a tiny embryo growing inside.

Growing seeds

In order to germinate, or develop into a plant, a seed needs water, oxygen and a reasonable temperature (not below freezing point). Seeds can germinate without soil. You could try growing some cress on damp blotting paper or cotton wool.

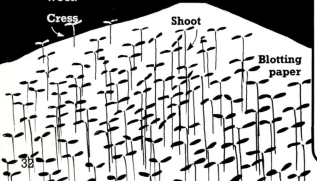

Cress — Shoot

Blotting paper

Plant life cycles

The life cycles of many plants are adapted to suit their climates and surroundings. Winters, or dry periods, can be tough on plants, so they have ways of becoming dormant. They stop feeding and growing and all their activities are slowed down until spring.

Annuals

Many garden flowers are annuals. This means that they live for one year only, growing and flowering in the warm period. In winter the leaves and flowers die, but the seeds remain to grow into new plants.

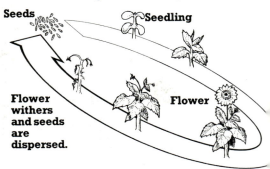

Seeds

Seedling

Flower withers and seeds are dispersed.

Flower

Seeds are well-adapted to survive winter. Their hard coat keeps out the cold. Their food store keeps them alive until spring, when they can produce leaves of their own and start carrying out photosynthesis.

Perennials

Trees and shrubs, such as roses, are perennials. They live for many years, as well as making seeds for new plants. In winter many become dormant. Their leaves drop off, which stops them losing water by transpiration. This means they can't carry out photosynthesis, so they live on stores of food in the stem and roots.

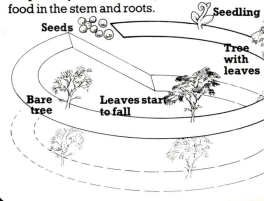

Seeds

Seedling

Tree with leaves

Bare tree

Leaves start to fall

Some animal life cycles

Some animals, such as insects and frogs, change their form several times in the course of their life cycle. This is called metamorphosis. These different stages can help the animal by providing a form in which it can survive the winter. The animal often feeds on different foods at different stages, which helps avoid competition for food between parents and young.

Butterfly's life cycle

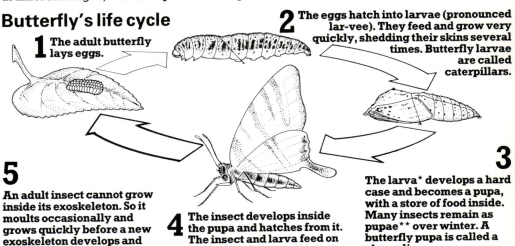

1 The adult butterfly lays eggs.

2 The eggs hatch into larvae (pronounced lar-vee). They feed and grow very quickly, shedding their skins several times. Butterfly larvae are called caterpillars.

3 The larva* develops a hard case and becomes a pupa, with a store of food inside. Many insects remain as pupae** over winter. A butterfly pupa is called a chrysalis.

4 The insect develops inside the pupa and hatches from it. The insect and larva feed on different things.

5 An adult insect cannot grow inside its exoskeleton. So it moults occasionally and grows quickly before a new exoskeleton develops and hardens.

Grasshopper's life cycle

Dragonflies, grasshoppers and some other insects, have only three stages in their life cycle.

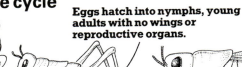

Eggs

Eggs hatch into nymphs, young adults with no wings or reproductive organs.

Adult

Frog's life cycle

A frog is another animal that undergoes metamorphosis. It takes about four months from egg to frog.

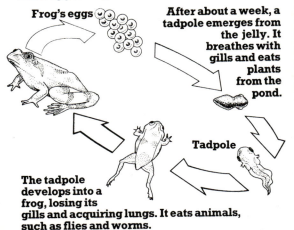

Frog's eggs

After about a week, a tadpole emerges from the jelly. It breathes with gills and eats plants from the pond.

Tadpole

The tadpole develops into a frog, losing its gills and acquiring lungs. It eats animals, such as flies and worms.

Watch a fly's life cycle

If you want to study the life cycle of a fly, you could capture some flies and leave them in a jar with some meat.

A complete cycle can take only 21 days.

Muslin lid, or tin with holes for breathing.

Meat for eggs to be laid on and for larvae to eat.

Sugar and food scraps for flies to eat.

*The singular of larvae.
**Pronounced pew-pee, the plural of pupa.

Genetics and heredity

What makes you take after your parents? Some of the similarities may be due to your upbringing and environment, but many others, such as the colour of your eyes, are inherited. Characteristics like these are controlled by instructions called genes. The study of genes, and the rules that decide which features you inherit from which parent, is called genetics.

Where are your genes?

Genes are spread out along thin, thread-like structures called chromosomes, which are in the nucleus of every cell. Chromosomes come in pairs. The number of pairs depends on the organism. Some plants have over 100 pairs of chromosomes in every cell; one species of worm has only one. Human beings have 23 pairs (or 46 chromosomes) in each cell.

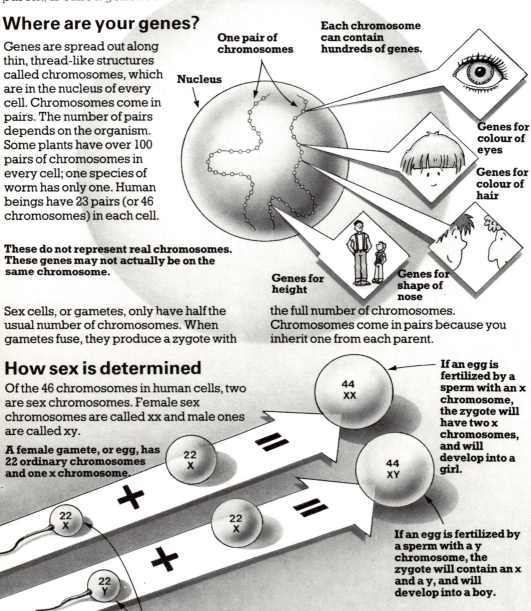

One pair of chromosomes

Each chromosome can contain hundreds of genes.

Nucleus

Genes for colour of eyes

Genes for colour of hair

Genes for shape of nose

Genes for height

These do not represent real chromosomes. These genes may not actually be on the same chromosome.

Sex cells, or gametes, only have half the usual number of chromosomes. When gametes fuse, they produce a zygote with the full number of chromosomes. Chromosomes come in pairs because you inherit one from each parent.

How sex is determined

Of the 46 chromosomes in human cells, two are sex chromosomes. Female sex chromosomes are called xx and male ones are called xy.

A female gamete, or egg, has 22 ordinary chromosomes and one x chromosome.

22 X

22 X

=

44 XX

If an egg is fertilized by a sperm with an x chromosome, the zygote will have two x chromosomes, and will develop into a girl.

22 X

22 X

=

44 XY

If an egg is fertilized by a sperm with a y chromosome, the zygote will contain an x and a y, and will develop into a boy.

22 Y

A male gamete, or sperm, may contain either an x or a y chromosome, in addition to the 22 other ones.

The 46 chromosomes in the zygote contain all the instructions necessary for all the cells in the body. The zygote develops by cell division, passing an exact copy of these instructions to each new cell.

What are genes made of?

Genes are composed of sections of the chemical DNA (deoxyribonucleic acid), which controls the activities in all living cells. Its structure was first discovered in Cambridge in 1953, by James Crick and Francis Watson.

Each molecule* of DNA is shaped in a double helix – like two spiral staircases wound round each other.

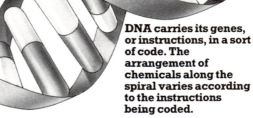

DNA carries its genes, or instructions, in a sort of code. The arrangement of chemicals along the spiral varies according to the instructions being coded.

Each step in the spiral consists of one of these two pairs.

DNA contains four other chemicals linked in pairs – adenine and thymine, cytosine and guanine.

How genes were discovered

The idea of genes, or factors, as he called them, was first worked out in 1865 by Gregor Mendel, a Czech monk. He experimented with breeding pea plants, working out how characteristics such as height and colour were inherited.

Dominant and recessive genes

Your cells contain at least two genes for each characteristic – one from each parent – but these are very often in conflict with one another. For instance, you might inherit a gene for brown eyes from your mother, and one for blue eyes from your father. What determines what your eye colour will be? Mendel solved this by discovering that one gene is often hidden by the other. The hidden gene is called "recessive", and the one that hides it is called "dominant".

In sweet peas, white is a recessive colour and red is a dominant one. Biologists show this by writing a capital "R" for red and a small letter "r" for white.

If you breed from two plants with Rr genes, their offspring will probably be in a ratio of three red to one white. Follow this diagram to see why.

If you breed from a red and a white plant, the new plants will all be red. But they will each have one R (red) and one r (white) gene.

To have recessive characteristics, offspring must receive a recessive gene from both parents.

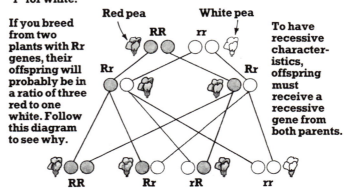

Red pea | White pea
RR | rr
Rr | Rr
RR | Rr | rR | rr

Genetic puzzle

Try to work out what will happen if you mate a spotted rabbit, with two dominant genes (SS), with a black rabbit, with two recessive genes (ss). What colour will their offspring be? And if one of them were mated with a rabbit with identical genes, what colour, or colours, would their offspring be?

*A molecule is the smallest part of a substance that can normally exist by itself.

Organizing biology

In order to make biology easier to study, biologists divide living organisms into groups with similar characteristics. They use the system of classification drawn up in the 18th century by the Swedish botanist, Karl von Linne. Living organisms are first divided into the animal and plant kingdoms*. Each animal and plant belongs to a species and has a species name, which consists of two words in Latin. A species is a group of organisms that are similar to each other and can breed together. Humans are one species; dogs are another. Each species belongs to a series of larger groups, as you can see in the chart below. A phylum is a main group and a class is a sub-group.

KINGDOM

PHYLUM

CLASS

ORDER

FAMILY

GENUS

SPECIES

*Some biologists consider a third kingdom, called protista, which groups together fungi, algae and many one-celled animals and plants.

The plant kingdom

Here you can find out about the main groups and classes in the plant kingdom.

1 Algae

Algae are very simple plants with no stems, roots or leaves. They grow in very wet or damp places. Seaweed and pondweed are types of algae.

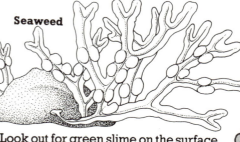

Seaweed

Look out for green slime on the surface of ponds. This is probably spirogyra, an algae made up of lots of single cells held together in threads.

7 Flowering plants

Flowering plants are also seed-bearing plants. They include trees as well as flowers. Their seeds are produced inside a fruit, which develops from a flower. Flowering plants are the most advanced, complex kind of plant.

2 Fungi

Fungi are unlike other plants as they are not green and cannot make their own food. Instead they feed off dead or decaying plants and animals. Many fungi are made up of tiny threads called hyphae (pronounced high-fee). Mushrooms, mildews and moulds are all types of fungi.

Spore cases containing spores

Hyphae

Grow your own bread mould

You could try growing mould on a piece of bread. Wet the bread and leave it for a few hours. Spores in the air will settle on it to feed and grow. Then cover it with a jar. Mould should develop within a few days. Cut off a piece and use a magnifying glass to see the details.

What moulds can do

There are both harmful and useful varieties of mould. Some moulds rot food or clothes, or cause diseases. Others can be used as antibiotics or for making the blue veins in cheeses.

3 Mosses and liverworts

Mosses and liverworts are slightly more complex plants with very thin leaves and no proper roots. They reproduce by spores. You can find mosses and liverworts growing in clusters, close to the ground, in wet or damp areas. If you look closely at mosses, you will see that they are made up of hundreds of tiny, separate plants.

Why do you think that simple plants, such as mosses and liverworts, always grow in damp areas, close to the ground?

5 Seed-bearing plants

Seed-bearing plants have roots, stems and leaves, and reproduce by means of seeds. Unlike a spore, a seed is made up of many cells. There are two classes of seed-bearing plant.

6 Conifers

Conifers are a class of seed-bearing plants. They have needle-shaped leaves and their seeds are produced in cones.

4 Ferns

Ferns are plants which have stems, leaves and roots, but no flowers. They grow in moist, shady places, such as woods. If you look at the backs of the leaves, you will see lots of dark spots. These contain the spores from which they reproduce.

The animal kingdom

In this section you can find out about some of the main classes and phyla of the animal kingdom. Mammals, birds, fish, reptiles and amphibians are all vertebrates. The simplest animals are called invertebrates, which means that they have no solid internal skeleton.

You may be able to find a variety of invertebrates to study just by looking in a garden or a park. You could try to find out what species they belong to, what they eat, what living conditions they like, when they are active (day or night) and how they move.

Protozoa

One-celled animals, such as amoebae, belong to the protozoa phylum. Protozoa usually live in water – in the sea, in ponds or in damp places, such as puddles – but you need a microscope to be able to see them.

Coelenterates

Coelenterates (pronounced see-lenterates) are animals with soft, hollow bodies and tentacles. Jellyfish, sea anemones and hydra are all coelenterates.

Arthropods

Arthropods have an exoskeleton, jointed legs and antennae. Their bodies are usually divided into three sections – head, thorax and abdomen. There are four main classes of arthropod.

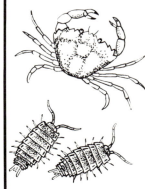

Crustaceans

Woodlice and shellfish, such as crabs and prawns are crustacea. They have between 10 and 14 legs, two pairs of antennae, and they respire by means of gills.

Arachnids

Spiders and scorpions are arachnids. They have eight legs, no antennae, and simple rather than compound eyes. Some arachnids spin webs for trapping their food.

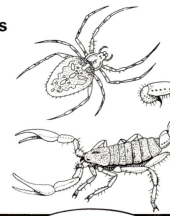

Annelids

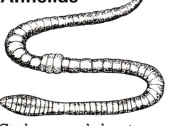

Garden worms belong to a phylum called annelids. They have soft bodies, divided into rings or segments. Worms move by relaxing and contracting muscles in their bodies.

Molluscs

Molluscs are soft-bodied animals with shells and a single foot. Snails, slugs and mussels are all molluscs.

If you find a snail, you could mark its shell with paint, and put it back outside. Then you could watch its movements to find out what kind of habitat it likes or how far it travels in a day.

Insects

Insects have six legs, two pairs of wings, two antennae and two compound eyes. Did you know that about 70% of all animals are insects?

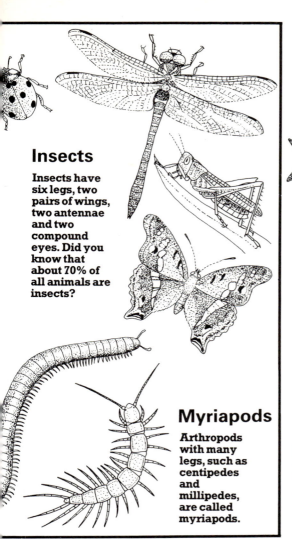

Myriapods

Arthropods with many legs, such as centipedes and millipedes, are called myriapods.

Echinoderms

Echinoderms are spiny-skinned animals, such as starfish and sea urchins.

Vertebrates

All animals with a backbone are called vertebrates.

Fish

Fish are cold-blooded vertebrates. They have scales and fins, breathe with gills and live in water.

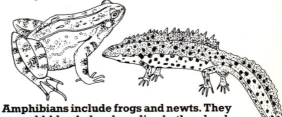

Amphibians

Amphibians include frogs and newts. They are cold-blooded and can live both on land and in water. They lay eggs in water.

Reptiles

Reptiles include snakes, lizards and turtles. They have scaly skin and lay eggs with shells on land.

Birds

Birds have feathers and wings and reproduce by laying eggs.

Mammals

Mammals are warm-blooded vertebrates with hair. They have lungs and two pairs of limbs and they feed their young with milk.

Classification computer program

If you have a microcomputer, or can borrow one, you could use this program to help you classify an animal. Think of an animal, then answer the questions to find out which phylum it belongs to. In some cases you can find out its class and order too. The program is written to work on a Commodore 64 or VIC 20 microcomputer. Lines that need changing for other computers are marked with a symbol and printed at the end of the program. Each symbol corresponds to a different computer. They are:

▲ **BBC**   ■ **ZX SPECTRUM**   ● **APPLE**

```
 10 GOSUB 380
 20 LET N=1
 30 GOSUB 320
 40 IF N<=NQ THEN GOSUB 140:GOTO 60
 50 IF N>100 THEN GOSUB 210
 60 IF N=999 THEN GOTO 120
 70 IF N<>0 THEN GOTO 40
 80 PRINT:PRINT "DO YOU WANT TO CLASSIFY ANOTHER ANIMAL"
 90 PRINT:GOSUB 300
100 IF A$="Y" THEN GOTO 20
110 PRINT "BYE...":STOP
120 PRINT:PRINT "SORRY - WE CANNOT CLASSIFY YOUR ANIMAL"
130 GOTO 80
140 GOSUB 280
■150 PRINT B$(S(N));" ";
160 RESTORE:FOR I=1 TO N:READ M$:NEXT I
170 PRINT M$:PRINT:PRINT:GOSUB 300
180 IF A$="Y" THEN LET N=Y(N)
190 IF A$="N" THEN LET N=N(N)
200 RETURN
210 GOSUB 280:GOSUB 360
220 FOR I=1 TO N-100:READ M$:NEXT I
230 PRINT "YOU HAVE A MEMBER OF THE ";M$
240 LET N=L(N-100):GOSUB 260:RETURN
250 GOSUB 260:RETURN
260 PRINT:PRINT "PRESS RETURN TO CONTINUE"
270 INPUT A$:RETURN
▲■280 PRINT CHR$(147)
290 RETURN
300 PRINT "ANSWER Y/N"
310 INPUT A$:RETURN
320 GOSUB 280:PRINT "THINK OF AN ANIMAL":PRINT
330 PRINT "ANSWER THESE QUESTIONS TO"
340 PRINT "CLASSIFY IT"
350 GOSUB 260:RETURN
360 RESTORE:FOR I=1 TO NQ:READ M$
370 NEXT I:RETURN
380 LET NQ=19:LET NS=19:GOSUB 360
■390 DIM Y(NQ):DIM N(NQ):DIM L(NS):DIM S(NQ):DIM B$(4)
400 FOR I=1 TO NS:READ M$:NEXT I
```

How to adapt the program

This is a very simple program, but it will give you an idea of how biologists can use computers to help them classify living things. The program has been written so that you can adapt it if you want to. You can expand the program by including extra questions and statements to classify an animal in more detail.

To ask another question, look at line 3200. Which of these phrases does your question begin with? Insert a number at the end of line 3210. If the question begins with "Does it have", insert 1, if it begins with "Is it", insert 2, and so on. After line 1180, add a new line – 1190 – and the rest of your question. After line 2090, add line 2100 and your answer. If there are no further questions, add a 0 at the end of line 3100. If you want to ask a further question, insert the number of that question – probably 21. (There are 19 questions in the program as it stands.) You also need to adjust line 380. NQ stands for the number of questions in the program, and NS for the number of statements or answers.

40

```
410 FOR I=1 TO NQ:READ Y(I):READ N(I):NEXT I
420 FOR I=1 TO NS:READ L(I):NEXT I
430 FOR I=1 TO 4:READ B$(I):NEXT I
440 FOR I=1 TO NQ:READ S(I):NEXT I
450 RETURN

1000 DATA "A SOLID INTERNAL SKELETON"
1010 DATA "MADE ONLY OF ONE CELL"
1020 DATA "IN WATER AND HAVE STINGING TENTACLES"
1030 DATA "A SOFT BODY, DIVIDED INTO RINGS OR SEGMENTS"
1040 DATA "AN EXTERNAL SKELETON"
1050 DATA "TWO PAIRS OF ANTENNAE AND BETWEEN 10 AND 14 LEGS"
1060 DATA "8 LEGS AND NO ANTENNAE"
1070 DATA "6 LEGS AND 3 BODY SECTIONS"
1080 DATA "A LONG BODY AND MANY LEGS"
1090 DATA "A SOFT BODY ENCLOSED IN A SHELL"
1100 DATA "IN THE SEA AND HAVE A SPINY SKIN"
1110 DATA "IN WATER, HAVE SCALES AND BREATHE WITH GILLS"
1120 DATA "MOIST SKIN, LIVE ON LAND, BUT LAY ITS EGGS IN WATER"
1130 DATA "ON LAND, HAVE SCALY SKIN AND LAY EGGS WITH SHELLS"
1140 DATA "WINGS WITH FEATHERS"
1150 DATA "WARM BLOODED AND DOES IT SUCKLE ITS YOUNG WITH MILK"
1160 DATA "LAY EGGS"
1170 DATA "A POUCH"
1180 DATA "YOUNG WHICH DEVELOP INSIDE A PLACENTA"

2000 DATA "VERTEBRATE SUBPHYLUM (CHORDATA PHYLUM)"
2010 DATA "PHYLUM PROTOZOA","PHYLUM COELENTERATES"
2020 DATA "PHYLUM ANNELIDS","PHYLUM ARTHROPOD"
2030 DATA "CLASS CRUSTACEA","CLASS ARACHNIDS"
2040 DATA "CLASS INSECTS","MYRIAPOD CLASS"
2050 DATA "MOLLUSC PHYLUM","PHYLUM ECHINODERM"
2060 DATA "FISH CLASS","AMPHIBIAN CLASS"
2070 DATA "CLASS REPTILES","CLASS BIRDS"
2080 DATA "CLASS MAMMALS","MONOTREME FAMILY"
2090 DATA "MARSUPIAL FAMILY","EUTHERIAN FAMILY"

3000 DATA 101,2,102,3,103,4,104,5,105,10,106,7,107,8,108,9,109,999
3010 DATA 110,11,111,999,112,13,113,14,114,15,115,16,116,999
3020 DATA 117,18,118,19,119,999
3100 DATA 12,0,0,0,6,0,0,0,0,0,0,0,0,0,0,0,17,0,0,0
3200 DATA "DOES IT HAVE","IS IT","DOES IT LIVE","DOES IT"
3210 DATA 1,2,3,1,1,1,1,1,1,1,3,3,1,3,1,2,4,1,1
```

Below is a list of changes that will enable you to run this program on other computers too. These instructions need to be inserted into program in the relevant places.

■ 150 LET C$=B$(S(N))
■ 152 IF C$(LEN(C$))=" " THEN LET C$=C$
  (TO LEN(C$)-1):GOTO 152
■ 155 PRINT C$;" ";
● 280 HOME
▲■ 280 CLS:PRINT:PRINT
■ 390 Change DIM B$(4) to DIM B$(4,12)

Ecology and the environment

Ecology is the study of the relationship between animals and plants and their surroundings. A group of animals and plants that live together are known as a community. The place where they live is called their habitat. Sometimes a living organism, such as a tree, provides a habitat for other plants and animals. The organisms in a habitat compete with each other for survival. They also depend on each other in many ways, for feeding or reproducing. Biologists refer to a community and its habitat as an ecosystem.

Insects and birds make nests in the branches.

Caterpillars feed on the leaves.

A tree is a habitat. This one is in a tropical forest.

Plants, such as ferns, mosses and orchids, put down roots in the bark, or use the trunk as a means of support.

You could make a study of the plants and animals in a large tree.

Competing for light

Organisms can co-exist successfully if they don't have to compete with each other. For instance, in a wood most of the light is captured by the tallest trees. However some plants, such as bluebells, grow and flower in the spring, while the trees are still bare. By the time the trees are green, these plants have withered.

You could investigate the different plants competing with each other on a lawn. Grass can shield other plants by growing taller.

But in areas that are well trampled, plants with wide leaves, such as daisies, can stunt grass seedlings.

Living together

Some plants and animals depend on each other in very specific ways. If the relationship benefits both of them, it is called symbiosis. If it only benefits one of them, it is called commensalism. If the relationship harms one of the partners, it is called parasitism.

Flea

Louse

Mosquito

Lice, mosquitoes and fleas are all parasites. They get their food from the living bodies of other animals.

Sea anemones sometimes travel on the backs of hermit crabs. The crab is protected from attackers by the anemone's stinging tentacles. The anemone eats scraps of food left over by the crab.

Sea anemone

Hermit crab

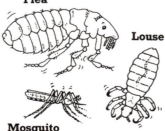

Food webs and chains

The animals and plants in a community are linked together into a complex food web. Increases in population are limited by the amount of food available, and by the fact that many organisms are eaten or die from disease. However, communities can change. If for some reason one species in a food web is wiped out, the rest of the web will be affected.

The organisms at the bottom of a food web are always more numerous than at the top. This is because the amount of energy passed along is reduced with each link in the chain. So biologists sometimes organize ecosystems into pyramids of feeding levels.

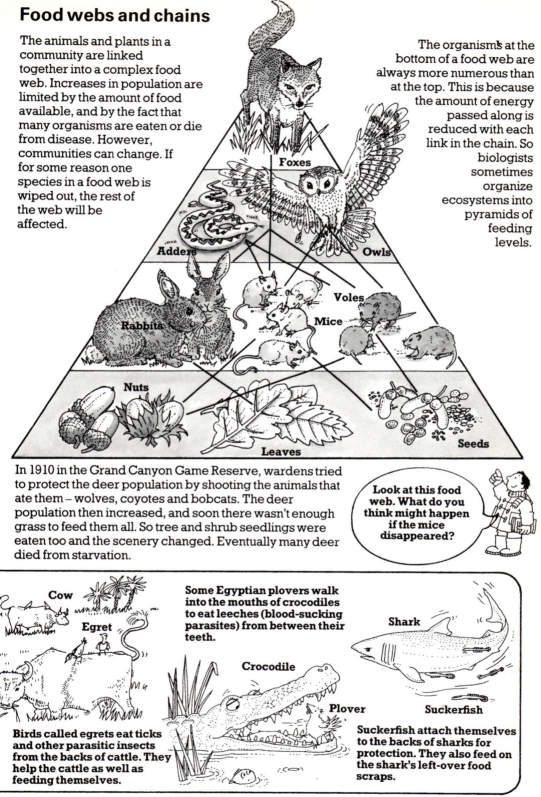

Foxes

Owls

Adders

Voles

Mice

Rabbits

Nuts

Leaves

Seeds

In 1910 in the Grand Canyon Game Reserve, wardens tried to protect the deer population by shooting the animals that ate them – wolves, coyotes and bobcats. The deer population then increased, and soon there wasn't enough grass to feed them all. So tree and shrub seedlings were eaten too and the scenery changed. Eventually many deer died from starvation.

Look at this food web. What do you think might happen if the mice disappeared?

Cow

Egret

Some Egyptian plovers walk into the mouths of crocodiles to eat leeches (blood-sucking parasites) from between their teeth.

Shark

Crocodile

Plover

Suckerfish

Birds called egrets eat ticks and other parasitic insects from the backs of cattle. They help the cattle as well as feeding themselves.

Suckerfish attach themselves to the backs of sharks for protection. They also feed on the shark's left-over food scraps.

What is pollution?

Pollution is the release of substances into the air, water or soil, which may kill or harm living organisms. There are many sources of pollution. Factories produce poisonous waste products which are released into the air as smoke, or flow into rivers and streams. Car exhausts also give off poisonous gases, and sewage can cause damage if it is dumped in rivers.

How rivers die

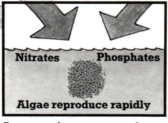

Nitrates   Phosphates

Algae reproduce rapidly

River with hardly any oxygen

Look out for green slime on the surface of rivers. This is made up of microscopic algae and is often a sign that a river is polluted.

Sewage, detergents and fertilizers all contain nitrates and phosphates which algae feed on. If these get into rivers, the algae reproduce rapidly.

When algae die, their bodies are broken down by bacteria. This process uses up oxygen. If the water loses a lot of oxygen, animals suffocate and die.

Lichen test

You can find lichens* on the barks of trees, walls and other surfaces. They are very sensitive to pollution, so you can use them as a rough guide to how polluted your area is. In very polluted areas, there are no lichens. The cleaner the air, the greater the variety of lichens.

Shrubby lichens

Grey, leafy lichens

Yellow-orange leafy lichens

Grey-green crusty lichens

No lichens. Only pleurococcus, a green, powdery alga.

Clean air   **Increasing pollution**   **Most pollution**

Acid test

You could try testing the acidity of the water in a local pond or stream. Use universal indicator papers. If the indicator number is less than 5, the water is unusually acid and may be polluted.

How people affect the environment

Humans can alter the environment in many ways. Cutting down forests, to make way for cities and farms, destroys the natural habitat of many organisms. So animals and plants have to compete for less and less territory. Pesticides, which farmers use to protect their crops, can upset food chains by destroying one of its links. Hunting, for food, clothing or cosmetic products has led to the extinction of many species.

44

*Lichens are produced by an alga and a fungus living together.
**You can buy these at a chemist's.

Competing for survival

Animals and plants produce large numbers of offspring, many of which are eaten or die before they reach maturity. Individuals within a species are never exactly alike, because of genetic differences. The ones that do survive tend to be stronger or better adapted for conditions in their environment. These characteristics are passed on, in their genes, to the next generation. In time, the characteristics of the unsuccessful individuals may die out. Biologists call this natural selection, or "survival of the fittest".

Which ones survive?

If an animal or plant is better camouflaged than other members of its species, it is less likely to be seen and eaten. ▼

▲ Many animals, such as deer, compete in order to mate. The strongest male wins and usually mates with all the females in the herd.

Those that are more resistant to disease or can run away from predators are also more likely to survive. ▼

Mutations

Sometimes, when a gamete is produced, a gene or chromosome is not copied properly. This leads to a variation, or mutation, in the instructions which produce the offspring. Most mutations are harmful. For instance, mongolism, or Down's syndrome, is the result of a mutation. However, if a mutation is beneficial, those individuals may survive to reproduce and may eventually outnumber the original variety.

Natural selection works very fast with bacteria, because they reproduce so rapidly. When a drug, such as penicillin, is used to kill bacteria, there are always a few immune bacteria which survive. These reproduce and the next generation of bacteria inherits immunity and so the drug becomes useless.

The case of the peppered moth

Peppered moths are usually pale and speckled and hide on lichens. There is also a black variety, which until the industrial revolution in about 1850, was extremely rare in Britain. Then smoke from factories blackened the trees and killed the lichens, so the pale moths were no longer so well camouflaged. By 1895, black moths had increased to 98% of the population in industrial areas.

Artificial selection

Farmers can use a knowledge of genetics to improve their crops and animals. For instance there might be a cow that produced a lot of milk but had a low resistance to disease, and another variety that was resistant to disease, but didn't produce much milk. Provided that the beneficial characteristics were controlled by dominant genes, a new and better type of cow could be produced by breeding from the two varieties.

Using a microscope

If you've got a microscope, you could use it to investigate different parts of animals and plants. With most ordinary home microscopes, you can magnify things to about 400 times their size (×400). The field ion or electron microscopes that some scientists use can get a magnification of about ×1,000,000. An ordinary magnifying glass will magnify things to about 10 times their size. Here are some ideas for things you could look at and equipment that you will need.

Scalpel for cutting thin slices from specimens. If you haven't got one, you could use a razor blade, but be extremely careful not to cut yourself.

Bread board or old tile for cutting on.

Stains are used to help you see the different parts of a specimen more clearly. Some parts absorb more of a stain than others. You could use iodine or kitchen food dyes.

Tweezers for picking up delicate specimens.

Dropper for applying liquid.

Looking at cells

You can get a sample of cheek cells by scraping the inside of your cheek with a finger. Put the liquid on a slide and add a drop of stain.

Cheek cells

To look at plant cells, you could mount a moss leaf in water. You should be able to see the cells and the green pigment inside the chloroplasts.

Moss cells

Grow a pollen tube

Collect some pollen and mount it on a slide with a drop of sugar solution. (Add a teaspoonful of sugar to half a cup of water.) After about an hour, look to see if the pollen has germinated and grown a tube*.

Pollen grain

Pollen tube

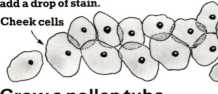

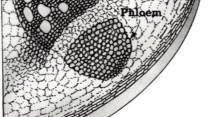

Xylem

Phloem

Looking at xylem tubes

If you cut a thin slice off a stem, you could investigate the xylem vessels. Leave the stem in coloured water first**, so that the xylem shows up clearly. Mount the slice in water.

Looking at stomata

If you coat a leaf with nail varnish, then peel the varnish off when it's dry, you will get a copy of the surface of the leaf. If you put this under the microscope, you should be able to see the shape of the stomata.

Petals

Looking for colour

You could try to find out where the colour is located in petals, or in coloured stems, such as rhubarb. Is the cytoplasm coloured, or is the colour contained in structures like chloroplasts?

*This is not always successful. If it doesn't work, you could try solutions of different strengths. **See the experiment on page 20.

Microscopic organisms

Pondwater contains numbers of microscopic organisms, such as amoebae. You could collect a bucket of pondwater and try a few drops at a time under the microscope. Here are a few of the organisms that you might see.

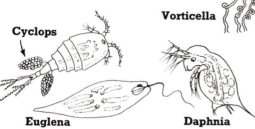

Vorticella

Cyclops

Euglena

Daphnia

Looking at insects

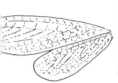

If you find dead insects, or other invertebrates, you could look at parts of their bodies, such as wings.

Answers to puzzles

Page 7: Why isn't a car a living thing?

A car isn't a living thing because it cannot grow or reproduce itself.

Page 9

Fungi are plants that do not contain chlorophyll. Most other plants contain chlorophyll even if they are not green.

Some adult sea animals, such as corals, sponges, barnacles and sea anemones, are not capable of locomotion, although they can move when they are very young.

Page 13: Monkey puzzle

Tree-living animals, such as monkeys, have forward-pointing eyes to help them judge distances accurately, as they jump from tree to tree.

Page 16

When you do a lot of exercise, you use up extra energy. To get this energy your cells respire faster and use up oxygen more quickly. You pant in order to take in extra oxygen to compensate for this.

Page 19

Your heart beats faster during exercise in order to speed up the flow of oxygen and food to the cells. This gives the cells more energy, so that your body can work harder.

Page 20

Cacti have narrow spines as leaves in order to reduce the surface area from which water may be lost. Cacti live in dry places, such as deserts, where water is scarce.

Trees lose their leaves in winter to avoid losing too much water by transpiration. If the ground is frozen, it may be difficult for the roots to take in water.

Page 26

Sneezing and blinking are both reflex actions.

Page 31

If a bacteria divided once every 20 minutes, after 10 hours there would be 905,969,664 bacteria. Bacteria do not actually increase at this rate, because many are eaten or do not survive.

Page 35: Genetics puzzle

If a black rabbit with two recessive black genes were mated with a spotted rabbit with two dominant spotted genes, all their offspring would be spotted. Each of the offspring would be spotted and would have one black gene and one spotted gene. If two rabbits of this kind were mated, they would produce three spotted rabbits for every one black one.

Page 45

Many simple plants grow in damp areas close to the ground because they don't have proper root and stem systems. This means that they cannot efficiently transport water and other substances through their bodies.

Page 43

If all the mice disappeared, the numbers of owls might decrease because of food shortages. Or the owls might turn to another source of food, such as voles, whose population would then get smaller.

Index